Animals in Danger

in South America

Louise and Richard Spilsbury

Heinemann
LIBRARY
Chicago, Illinois

Edited by Rebecca Rissman, Dan Nunn, and Adrian Vigliano
Designed by Philippa Jenkins
Picture research by Tracy Cummins
Originated by Capstone Global Library Ltd.
Printed in China by South China Printing Company, Ltd.

17 16 15 14 13
10 9 8 7 6 5 4 3 2 1

Library of Congress Cataloging-in-Publication Data
Cataloging-in-Publication data is on file at the Library of Congress.
ISBN: 978-1-4329-7677-4 (HC) 978-1-4329-7684-2 (PB)

Acknowledgments
The author and publisher are grateful to the following for permission to reproduce copyright material: Alamy p. 9 (© National Geographic Image Collection); Getty Images pp. 27 (Gunter Ziesler), 28 (Roevin); National Geographic Stock p. 10 (FRED BAVENDAM/MINDEN PICTURES); Newscom pp. 14 (EPA/RUDOLF VON MAY), 19 (Malcolm Schuyl/FLPA), 29 (Daniel Beltra/Greenpeace); Photo Researchers, Inc. p. 18 (Mark Bowler); Shutterstock pp. 4 (© Chris P.), 5 left (© Pichugin Dmitry), 5 right (© GlobetrotterJ), 6 (© Pal Teravagimov), 15 (© Eric Gevaert), 17 (© Carles Fortuny), 23 (© AISPIX by Image Source), 25 (© Tim Grootkerk), 29 inset (© vblinov), icons (© Florian Augustin), (© tristan tan), maps (© AridOcean); Superstock pp. 11 (© Michael S. Nolan / age footstock), 13, 22, 26 (© Minden Pictures), 21 (© Juniors).

Cover photograph of a jaguar reproduced with permission of Shutterstock (© Karen Givens).
Cover photograph of a yellow anaconda reproduced with permission of Shutterstock (© JoeFotoSS).
Cover photograph of a golden lion tamarin baby reproduced with permission of Shutterstock (© Eric Gevaert).
Cover photograph of a tropical blue parrot reproduced with permission of istockphoto (© Arthur Carlo Franco).

We would like to thank Michael Bright for his invaluable help in the preparation of this book.

Contents

Some words are shown in bold, **like this.** You can find out what they mean by looking in the glossary.

Where Is South America?

We divide the world into seven large areas of land called **continents**. You can see them on the map of the world below. South America is the fourth-largest continent in the world.

NORTH AMERICA

EUROPE

ASIA

ATLANTIC OCEAN

PACIFIC OCEAN

AFRICA

PACIFIC OCEAN

SOUTH AMERICA

INDIAN OCEAN

N

W   E

S

AUSTRALIA

ANTARCTICA

Can you see the continent of South America?

In South America, there are huge rivers, thick forests, high mountains, and wide, flat **grasslands**. The Amazon **rain forest** is the largest in the world. The Andes is the world's highest **mountain range**!

It is sunny and wet in the Amazon rain forest, but much colder in the Andes mountains!

Animals of South America

Some animals in South America are **endangered**. There are very few of that type of animal left. If they all die, that type of animal will be **extinct**. Animals that are extinct are gone from the planet forever!

Hunters kill jaguars like this one to sell their beautiful fur.

Different types of animals look and behave differently from each other. We sort them into groups to help tell them apart.

Animal Classification Chart

Amphibian	• lives on land and in water • has damp, smooth skin • has **webbed** feet • lays many eggs	
Bird	• has feathers and wings • hatches out of hard-shelled eggs	
Fish	• lives in water • has **fins** and most have **scales** • young hatch from soft eggs	
Mammal	• drinks milk when a baby • has hair on its body	
Reptile	• has scales on its body • lives on land • young hatch from soft-shelled eggs	

Look out for pictures like these next to each photo. They will tell you what type of animal each photo shows.

The North

Some **endangered** animals in the northern part of South America live in **mangrove** forests or on islands. Mangrove trees grow in shallow water by the coast. People cut them down to build hotels, homes, and farms.

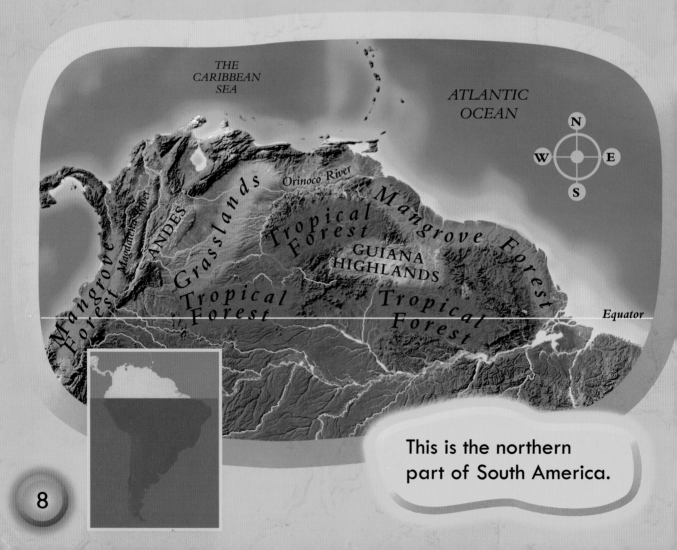

THE CARIBBEAN SEA

ATLANTIC OCEAN

N
W   E
S

Orinoco River

Mangrove Forest

Magdalena River

ANDES

Grasslands

Tropical Forest

Mangrove Forest

GUIANA HIGHLANDS

Tropical Forest

Tropical Forest

Equator

This is the northern part of South America.

8

Young rainbow parrotfish hatch from eggs among mangrove roots. They are safe from **predators** here, and there is lots of food for them to eat. Without mangroves, baby fish have nowhere to grow.

Rainbow parrotfish scrape off bits of plants to eat with teeth like a parrot's beak!

A manatee has to eat a lot of plants to fill itself up!

West Indian manatees swim along the coast, eating sea grass and other plants. People destroy the grass when they build on the coast. Some manatees also get hit by tourist and fishing boats.

This giant tortoise lives only on the Galapagos Islands. It is endangered because of the animals people have brought there. Cats and dogs eat young tortoises before their shell is hard enough to protect them.

The Galapagos giant tortoise is a giant—it can be almost 5 feet (1.5 meters) long!

The Amazon Rain Forest

It's hot and rainy all year in the Amazon **rain forest**. That's why trees here are some of the tallest on Earth! People cut down trees to build farms and houses on the land and to sell the wood.

Tropical Forest

Equator

Rio Negro

Amazon River

Tropical Forest

Rio Madeira

Rio Xingu

Tropical Forest

Area where trees have been cut down

PACIFIC OCEAN

N W E S

MATO GROSSO PLATEAU

This map shows the Amazon rain forest in South America.

Harpy eagles only have one chick every two to three years!

Harpy eagles need rain forests to survive. They snatch monkeys, birds, and other **prey** from trees with their long, sharp claws. They make nests high in the treetops so that chicks are safe from **predators.**

Oxapampa poison frogs can release deadly poisons through their skin! The frogs eat ants that eat poisonous rain forest plants. Then the frogs use the poison to kill predators that try to attack them!

The poison frog's bright colors warn predators that it is deadly, so they leave it alone!

The golden lion tamarin got its name because of its lion-like mane of hair.

Golden lion tamarins rely on trees, too. They eat fruit, **insects**, and small lizards in trees during the day. They use their long fingers to pull prey from cracks in the **bark**. They sleep in tree holes at night.

The Andes Mountains

The Andes Mountains run down the western side of South America. People change animal **habitats** here to build farms, homes, and roads. They also dig **mines** for metals such as tin and copper.

Tropical Forest

Mount Huascaran (6,768 meters)

Area where trees have been cut down

Ucayali River

ANDES MOUNTAINS

Lake Titicaca

Lake Poopo

PACIFIC OCEAN

Mount Aconcagua (6,960 meters)

N W E S

The Andes mountain range is 5,500 miles (8,900 kilometers) long!

Andean condors soar over mountaintops looking for dead animals below. They have sharp, hooked beaks to eat their **prey**. Farmers shoot condors because they think the birds kill farm animals.

Mountain winds help heavy Andean condors to fly!

This monkey gets its name from the small yellow band on the underside of its tail.

The yellow tailed wooly monkey has long, thick hair. This keeps it warm in the high, cold mountain forests where it lives. Sadly, people cut down the trees they live in to sell and to clear land for roads and farms.

Chinchillas have thick, silky fur to keep them warm on mountains. They rest in holes in rocks during the day and eat plants at night. Today, they are under threat because people cut down plants where they live.

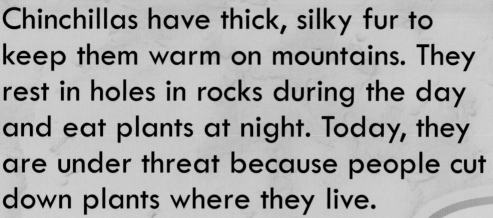

People once hunted chinchillas to use their fur to make coats.

Central Wetlands

Wetlands are areas of shallow water by trees. Some **wetlands** in central South America are changing. **Pollution** washes into wetlands from **mines**, fields, and towns. People clear trees for farms.

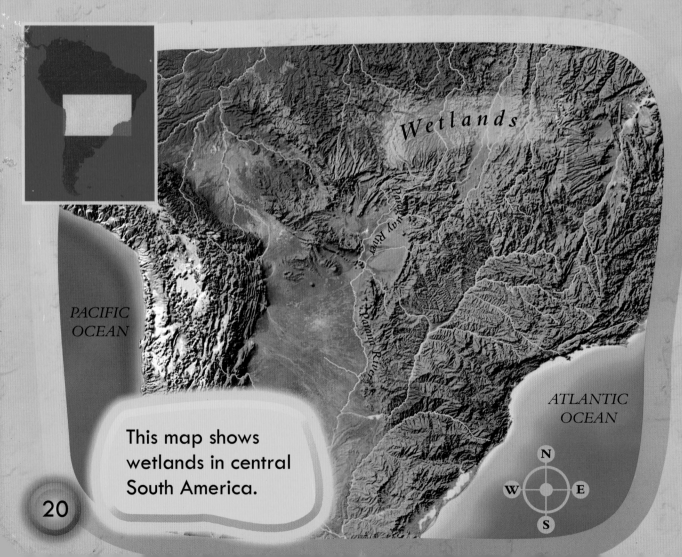

Wetlands

Paraguay River

Paraná River

PACIFIC OCEAN

ATLANTIC OCEAN

This map shows wetlands in central South America.

Giant otters use **webbed** feet and a large tail to swim fast through wetlands. They catch fish, snakes, and other animals using their sharp teeth. Sadly, pollution kills the fish that they eat.

Giant otter pups can swim when they are only two weeks old!

A hyacinth macaw's big, strong beak can crack open even the hardest nuts!

Hyacinth macaws live in wetland trees. They eat nuts from trees and make nests in trees. They lose their homes and food when people clear trees for cattle ranches. People capture them to sell as pets, too.

The yellow anaconda's spotted skin helps it hide in forests and murky water. Then it attacks. It wraps its body around birds and other animals and squeezes to kill them. Then it swallows them whole!

People hunt anacondas for their skin and to sell as pets or to zoos.

Southeast Pampas

In the southeast there are lots of pampas **grasslands**. Some animals here are **endangered** because of **habitat** loss. The soil is good in some places, so farmers clear lots of grasslands to grow **crops** on.

Farmland

Paraná River

Uruguay River

Plate River

Pampas Grassland

Pampas Grassland

ANDES MOUNTAINS

PACIFIC OCEAN

ATLANTIC OCEAN

N
W   E
S

Many kinds of animals live in the pampas grasslands.

The maned wolf eats fruit and small animals. Its huge ears hear **prey** when it hunts at night. Then it pounces on prey to catch it. With fewer plants, there is less fruit and less prey for wolves to eat.

The maned wolf's very long legs help it to see over tall grasses in the pampas!

The lesser rhea eats mainly grass and seeds, but also bugs and **insects**, too.

The lesser rhea is a huge bird that cannot fly. It has long, powerful legs to run away from danger! It feeds in grasslands. Its habitat is cleared for farming, and people kill it for meat and feathers.

A giant armadillo has tough body armor made from hard **scales**. It uses its huge, sharp claws to dig burrows to rest in during the day. At night, it digs into ant nests and **bark** to get insects to eat.

The giant armadillo is endangered because people take its land and hunt it for food.

Helping South America's Animals

One way to protect **endangered** animals is to protect their **habitats**. Some countries do this by making **reserves**. People cannot hunt or build in these areas of land, so animals can live safely there.

Humboldt's penguins are endangered but these animals are safe because they live in a protected area.

Save rain forests by eating Brazil nuts!

You can help South America's endangered animals, too! Buy and eat Brazil nuts. Then people won't cut down Brazil nut trees. Ask your family not to buy wooden furniture made from **rain forest** trees.

Glossary

bark outer covering of a tree

continent one of seven large areas that make up the world's land

crop food plant

endangered when a type of animal is in danger of dying out

extinct no longer alive; not seen in the wild for 50 years

fin flap of skin that helps a fish swim

grassland area of land mainly covered in grass

habitat place where plants and animals live

insect small animal with six legs, such as an ant or fly

mangrove tree that grows in shallow, muddy, salt water

mine deep hole in the ground people dig to get coal or metals

mountain range long line of mountains

pollution something that poisons or damages air, water, or land

predator animal that catches and eats other animals for food

prey animal that gets caught and eaten by other animals

rain forest forest of very tall trees, often found in hot, sunny, wet places

reserve large area of land where plants and animals are protected

scale small, overlapping pieces that cover an animal's body

webbed when feet have skin between the toes

wetland land covered in shallow water

Find Out More

Books

Allgor, Marie. *Endangered Animals of South America.*
New York: PowerKids Press, 2011.

Kalman, Bobbie. *Why Do Animals Become Extinct*?
New York: Crabtree Publishing Co., 2012.

Internet sites

Facthound offers a safe, fun way to find web sites
related to this book. All the sites on Facthound have
been researched by our staff.

Here's all you do:
Visit www.facthound.com
Type in this code: 9781432976774

Index